A Note to Par

DK READERS is a compelling progra... ....g
readers, designed in conjunction with leading literacy
experts, including Dr. Linda Gambrell, Director of
the School of Education at Clemson University.
Dr. Gambrell has served on the Board of Directors
of the International Reading Association and as
President of the National Reading Conference.

Beautiful illustrations and superb full-color photographs
combine with engaging, easy-to-read stories to offer
a fresh approach to each subject in the series. Each
DK READER is guaranteed to capture a child's
interest while developing his or her reading skills,
general knowledge, and love of reading.

The four levels of DK READERS are aimed at
different reading abilities, enabling you to choose the
books that are exactly right for your child:

Level 1 – Beginning to read
Level 2 – Beginning to read alone
Level 3 – Reading alone
Level 4 – Proficient readers

The "normal" age at which a child begins to read
can be anywhere from three to eight years old, so these
levels are only a general guideline.

No matter which level you select,
you can be sure that you are helping
your child learn to read,
then read to learn!

LONDON, NEW YORK, MUNICH,
MELBOURNE, AND DELHI

**Edited and designed
by Nimbusbooks**

Senior Art Editor Clare Shedden
Series Editor Deborah Lock
U.S. Editor Regina Kahney
Production Shivani Pandey
Picture Researcher Angela Anderson
Illustrator Malcolm Chandler
Jacket Designer Karen Burgess
Indexer Lynn Bresler

Subject Consultant
Andy McNae, National Officer for
the British Mountaineering Council

Reading Consultant
Linda Gambrell, Ph.D.

First American Edition, 2001
11 12 13 14 10 9 8 7 6 5
Published in the United States by DK Publishing, Inc.
375 Hudson Street, New York, New York 10014
007-MB145P-March/2001

Published in Great Britain by Dorling Kindersley Limited

Library of Congress Cataloging-in-Publication Data
Donkin, Andrew-
 Danger on the Mountain / by Andrew Donkin. -- 1st American ed.
 p. cm. -- (Dorling Kindersley readers)
            ISBN-13: 978-0-7894-7385-1 (pbk)
            ISBN-13: 978-0-7894-7386-8 (plc)
 1. Mountaineering--History--Juvenile literature. [1. Mountaineering.]
I. Title. II. Series.
GV199.89 .D66 2001
796.52'2--dc21   00-055546

Color reproduction by Colourscan, Singapore
Printed and bound in China by L Rex Printing Co., Ltd.

The publisher would like to thank the following for their kind permission
to reproduce their images:
c=center; t=top; b=below; l=left; r=right
Chris Bonington Picture Library: 22. **Corbis UK Ltd:** 22-23, 40.
John Frost Historical Newspapers: 21inset. **Hulton Getty:** 17tr, 42.
Bill Hatcher: 31tr, 32. **Illustrated London News Picture Library:**
9cl, 10tl. **George Mallory II:** 46. **John Cleare / Mountain Camera:** 4tl,
5tr, 8tl, 18, 21 main picture, 26, 33; Colin Monteath 6-7, 9tr, 37.
Popperfoto: 25tr. **Rex Features:** 43, 45, 47. **Tony Stone Images:**
Front jacket; Dennis Oda 41tr. **Topham Picturepoint:** 6tl, 13tr,
15cr, 16, 16b, 36.
All other images © Dorling Kindersley
For further information see: www.dkimages.com

Discover more at
www.dk.com

Contents

Mountain wonder   4

The vanishing   6

Top of the world   14

Disaster on K2   22

The challenge   30

Alone in the night   36

A search for heroes   42

Glossary   48

DANGER on the MOUNTAIN

SCALING THE WORLD'S HIGHEST PEAKS

Written by Andrew Donkin

DK Publishing, Inc.

Avalanches
Loud noises or movement can cause huge blocks of snow to sweep down mountainsides. The sheer weight of snow can also cause avalanches.

Snow blindness
At great heights, the sun is very strong. As it beats down on the white snow, the glare created can literally blind people.

Mountain wonder

The world's highest mountains have always fascinated people. Ancient civilizations believed their snow-capped peaks were the homes of gods. Only in the last century have the highest peaks been explored and climbed.

Mountaineering is very exciting but also dangerous. Killer rockfalls and sweeping avalanches are constant threats.

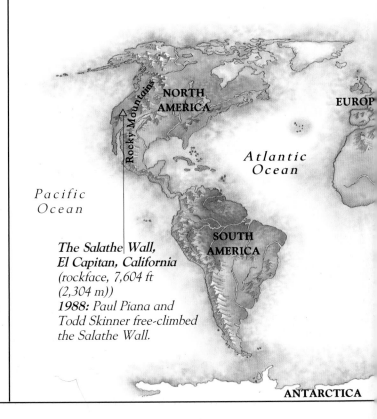

NORTH AMERICA

EUROPE

Rocky Mountains

Atlantic Ocean

Pacific Ocean

SOUTH AMERICA

The Salathe Wall, El Capitan, California (rockface, 7,604 ft (2,304 m))
1988: Paul Piana and Todd Skinner free-climbed the Salathe Wall.

ANTARCTICA

When scaling the highest peaks, climbers are prepared to risk mountain sickness, snow blindness, and frostbite. But the sheer excitement, sense of team spirit, and feeling of accomplishment outweigh any physical discomfort they experience.

In this book, you'll read some of the most exciting and courageous stories from the world of mountaineering. ❖

Mountain sickness
As you climb higher there is less oxygen in the air, causing headaches, dizziness, blurred vision, and exhaustion. This is known as mountain sickness.

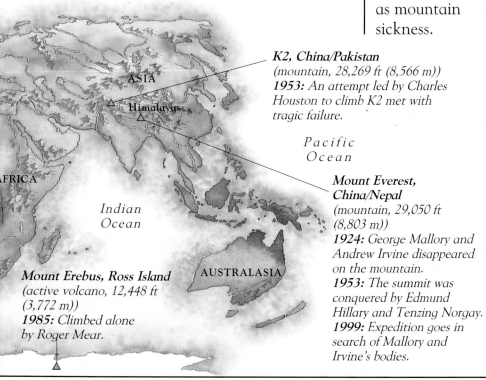

K2, China/Pakistan
(mountain, 28,269 ft (8,566 m))
1953: An attempt led by Charles Houston to climb K2 met with tragic failure.

Pacific Ocean

ASIA

Himalayas

AFRICA

Indian Ocean

AUSTRALASIA

Mount Erebus, Ross Island
(active volcano, 12,448 ft (3,772 m))
1985: Climbed alone by Roger Mear.

Mount Everest, China/Nepal
(mountain, 29,050 ft (8,803 m))
1924: George Mallory and Andrew Irvine disappeared on the mountain.
1953: The summit was conquered by Edmund Hillary and Tenzing Norgay.
1999: Expedition goes in search of Mallory and Irvine's bodies.

George Mallory
A former school teacher, Mallory visited Everest in 1921 and soon became obsessed with reaching its summit.

Scouting ahead
Mallory was a member of the British team that scouted Everest in 1921. The team returned in 1922 and two members climbed to within 1,740 ft (527 m) of the top before bad weather drove them back.

The vanishing

Date: May, 1924
Place: Mount Everest, Himalayas, Nepal-China border

Experienced mountaineer George Mallory looked up at the huge expanse of snow and rock filling the horizon. Mount Everest rose high up into the clouds. He was back.

Mallory had tried to climb Everest before, but terrible blizzards and exhaustion had beaten him. This time he was determined to reach the summit.

Mount Everest is 29,050 ft (8,803 m) above sea level!

Mount Everest is the highest mountain in the world, and a very dangerous and hostile place. No one can survive the freezing cold and thin air of its upper slopes for long.

When Mallory was asked why he wanted to climb Everest, he replied simply, "Because it's there."

Mallory began his expedition in 1924 with a visit to a local monastery to get a special blessing from the monks. Mallory knew that if he and his team were going to be the first to conquer Everest, they would need both weather and luck on their side.

Monastery
A monastery is a place where monks live. Monks are men who belong to a religious group and live apart from the rest of the community.

Himalayas
Mount Everest is part of the Himalayas – a mountain range that is 1,500 miles (2,414 kms) long! The Himalyas run across Asia.

Foothills
The lower slopes of a mountain are called foothills.

Porter
A porter is a local person hired to carry equipment up the mountainside.

Holy mountain
Chomolunga is the original Tibetan name for Mount Everest. It means "Goddess mother of the world."

Mallory and his team began their ascent, working up the foothills of the mountain. Porters carried most of the equipment. The team soon climbed above the snow line – the height at which snow and ice never melt, even in summer. Once past the snow line, the porters left and the team carried their own equipment.

The landscape changed as they left behind the gray rocks of the lower slopes. Now they walked across thick snow surrounded by walls of ice twisted into alien shapes.

When the slope became very steep, the men worked in pairs. One man climbed ahead, banging wooden pegs into the rock face. The pegs were hollow to make them lighter to carry. Safety ropes were attached to the secured pegs and the man behind climbed up using the ropes. Mallory paired up with Andrew Irvine.

8

Mallory always liked to lead from the front, but even he paused as they came to a 230-ft-(70-m)-high wall of perfectly smooth blue ice.

An artist's impression of Mallory on a step speaking to Irvine.

Clothing
Early climbers were very under-equipped by today's standards. They had only sweaters and tweed jackets to protect them from the cold! Today's climbers have special lightweight equipment to protect them.

Crampons
Crampons are metal spikes that are fitted to a climber's boots to give a better grip on ice and snow.

9

Oxygen tanks
The expedition carried oxygen to help them breathe in the thin air at the highest points. Unfortunately, the tanks were heavy and often leaked.

Ideal weather
Everest is hit by gales from November to March and by monsoons from June to September. The best time to climb the mountain is between April and early June.

The ice wall was nearly vertical. Finding a safe route up was a slow and dangerous task. It was difficult climbing with their thick gloves, but to remove them would certainly lead to frostbite. The men had to carry their tents, food, oxygen tanks, and other supplies up the ice wall, too.

At last they clambered over the top of the ice wall and collapsed on to the snow. When they had recovered, Mallory unroped himself from his climbing partner and went to scout the way ahead.

But as he stepped forward onto the thick snow covering the ground, it suddenly gave way beneath him! Mallory had fallen into a crevasse – a deep crack in the ice. He plummeted down into the depths of the crevasse until he came to an abrupt halt, breathless and nearly blind from the chunks of snow and ice that crashed into him.

Mallory's ice axe had caught on the side of the crevasse, stopping his fall. It had saved his life! Below him the crevasse fell away into darkness. Slowly and carefully, Mallory eased himself upward and climbed out.

The expedition was just one day's climb from the peak now, but the team's first two attempts to reach it failed due to poor weather.

On June 8th, with bad weather closing in, Mallory and Irvine set out for one last attempt. Mallory was determined to reach the peak.

Just before lunchtime, team member Noel Odell, watching the summit and surrounding area from far below, saw the clouds break apart for a few moments.

In the distance, he saw two tiny figures moving across the snow. Then the clouds closed in and they disappeared. It was the last time anyone ever saw George Mallory and Andrew Irvine alive.

The expedition waited for four agonizing days before returning home with the tragic news. Mallory and Irvine were dead. But had they reached the summit first? This question would haunt climbers on Everest for over 75 years. ❖

Andrew Irvine
Irvine was an engineering student at Oxford University in England. He had been on earlier expeditions to Everest.

Icefall
An icefall is very dangerous. It is created when a glacier falls steeply and creates many crevasses. An icefall moves constantly and huge blocks of ice tumble from it. Icefalls are often found on the lower slopes of mountains.

Glacier
A glacier is a huge body of thick, solid ice. It is formed by snow melting, refreezing, and compressing as more snow falls.

Solid ice moves like a river.

Cross-section of a glacier

Top of the world

Date: Summer, 1953
Place: Mount Everest, Himalayas, Nepal-China border

For 30 years after the disappearance of George Mallory and Andrew Irvine, Everest refused to be conquered. No one succeeded in reaching the summit.

In the early 1950s, a new route was discovered. This route led to the southwest face of Everest. But to get there, explorers had to travel over the Khumbu glacier and ascend its amazing 2,000-ft- (606-m)-high icefall.

An icefall is a dangerous maze of walls of ice, deep chasms, and twisting ice towers. Climbers have to struggle through hip-deep snowfalls just to reach the Khumbu icefall!

Legendary Yeti
Yeti are legendary half-man, half-ape creatures that the locals believe live on the slopes of Everest. They are said to be covered in reddish-brown hair.

While searching for a way up the icefall in 1951, climber Eric Shipton found a set of strange footprints in the snow. The Sherpa told him they were Yeti tracks – the legendary snowman of the Himalayas. Since then, others have reported seeing strange footprints in the snow, too.

Meanwhile, the new route up the Khumbu glacier and icefall was waiting to be conquered. And climbers were eager to try this new route.

Sherpas
Sherpas live on the borders of China and Nepal. They are used to living at high altitudes and are skilled mountaineers.

15

Swiss climbers attempted the new route twice in 1952. When both their expeditions failed due to bad weather, people wondered if the summit would ever be conquered.

The following year, in 1953, Colonel John Hunt was asked to lead a British expedition. He hand-picked his team of 14 men. Edmund Hillary and Tenzing Norgay were part of the team.

Hunt knew that training and preparation were vital if they were to succeed where all earlier expeditions had failed. The team needed time to adapt to the thin air so they did not get out of breath too quickly when climbing.

Hunt tested the team and their oxygen tanks by making them climb Everest's surrounding peaks. "We're going to spend the next two weeks climbing as many 20,000-ft (6,000-m) peaks around here as we can!" ordered Hunt.

Tenzing Norgay Tenzing began working on Everest as a Sherpa but soon became a well-respected climber in his own right.

When they started their ascent, the team had to climb the much-feared Khumbu icefall. The icefall constantly broke up and moved. Huge blocks of ice fell at random. Could they find a safe route?

Tenzing with oxygen tanks used on the climb

Crevasse
A crevasse is a crack in the surface of a glacier. It can be very wide and deep. Crevasses must be crossed with great care using ropes, ladders, and sometimes natural snow bridges.

Base camp
The expedition set up base camp at the foot of the Khumbu icefall. Base camps are set up at the foot of difficult climbs.

The men carefully worked their way up the unstable icefall. They fixed safety ropes in a web over the slippery ice so that other team members could follow.

At many points, they had to swing across deep crevasses where the ice had split open. Sometimes they used rope ladders as makeshift bridges suspending them above the drop. At other points, roped up together, they had to cross crevasses on unstable snow bridges.

The men nicknamed some of the obstacles after the first climber who tackled them. One obstacle, Hillary's Horror, was a huge 40-ft-(12-m)-wide crevasse. The only way to cross it was by edging their way along a block of ice that was wedged in the top! Hillary felt the block tremble with each step.

It took the men four days to find a route up the icefall. Over the next week, they made it fairly safe by fixing ropes and ladders, so their porters could carry the supplies and equipment through the icefall.

Storing supplies
Climbers store a range of supplies at their camps, including food, climbing gear, medical supplies, and equipment for recording their expedition.

Finally, almost at the summit, the men knew only two people would be chosen for the final assault to the top. Hunt decided Charles Evans and Tom Bourdillon would try first. If they failed, Edmund Hillary and Tenzing Norgay would go.

Gales slowed down Evans and Bourdillon. When they were only 300 ft (90 m) from the summit, they realized they did not have enough oxygen to reach it and return safely.

It was now up to Hillary and Tenzing. Despite the awful weather, they made good progress at first. But as they climbed higher, the unstable snow became increasingly dangerous. The ridge before the peak was guarded by twisted, overhanging spikes of ice. The men edged their way along it. Any fall would be fatal!

At last they climbed over the ridge and up to the peak!

At 11:30 a.m. on May 29, 1953, Edmund Hillary and Tenzing Norgay stepped onto the summit of Everest, the highest mountain in the world. They had done it! ❖

Tenzing on the top of Everest, May 29, 1953

Front page of English newspaper "News Chronicle" on June 2, 1953

Disaster on K2

Date: Summer, 1953
Place: K2, Himalayas, northern Pakistan

Team leader
Charles Houston was well-qualified to lead an expedition – he started climbing with his father at the age of 12.

As Charles Houston sat in the tent listening to the storm getting steadily stronger, he wondered for the first time if the team was going to die. "Sounds like it's getting worse," said Bob Bates, from the back of the tent.

The two friends were members of an eight-man team led by Houston. They were attempting to be the first people to reach the snow-covered summit of K2 in the Himalayas, the second highest mountain in the world.

Houston had first visited K2 14 years earlier and had been waiting for a chance to return ever since.

That spring, he had carefully hand-picked a team he thought would be able to climb K2 – a mountain that many people said was more dangerous than Everest. The expedition had started well. The men were in good spirits as they climbed K2's lower slopes. But as they got higher, things started to go wrong.

K2 towers proudly at 28,269 ft (8,566 m) in the eastern Himalayas.

Deadly blizzards
A blizzard is a violent snowstorm during which winds often blast snow over 35 miles (56 kilometers) per hour. It is difficult, even impossible, to see during a blizzard. A single blizzard can last for many days.

The weather slowed their progress and their supplies were running low. As the team reached a height of 27,170 ft (8,233 m), a terrible blizzard hit the mountain, hurtling chunks of snow at them. The men set up camp and quickly crawled inside their tents for shelter.

That was four days ago and they had been trapped inside their tents ever since!

"When this storm passes," Houston told Bates, shouting against the terrible noise of the wind, "we should still be able to reach the summit and get down safely. All we have to do is wait!"

But disaster struck the next day. The storm did ease, but as the men crawled bleary-eyed out of their tents, team member Art Gilkey suddenly collapsed, unconscious!

Lost in 1939
During their climb, Houston and his team found an abandoned camp from a 1939 American expedition led by Fritz Wiessner. His team met with tragic failure – team member Dudley Wolfe died.

Dudley Wolfe
Although eager, Wolfe was a very poor climber. He had been invited to join the 1939 group because he was very rich and helped finance the climb.

Godwin-Austin Glacier
This is a huge glacier that lies along the east side of K2. It is named after Henry Haversham Godwin-Austin, one of the first Westerners to explore the area.

Dangerous clot
Having a blood clot was very dangerous for Gilkey. At any moment the clot could be carried to his lungs, which would kill him.

"It's my leg," Gilkey struggled to say as he came around. "It's been painful for a few days, but it will get better."

Sadly, Charles Houston could not agree. He examined Gilkey and discovered that he had a blood clot in his leg. They had to get him down the mountain as soon as possible or he would die.

As they started to descend the mountain slopes, everyone realized that this would be the most dangerous climb they had ever attempted.

Using a makeshift stretcher made from part of a tent, they headed down the powder-white snowfields, the whole team roped together. Progress was slow and exhausting.

Suddenly George Bell lost his footing on a patch of hard, slippery ice. He tumbled down the mountain, dragging the two closest team members with him.

The falling men crashed into Houston and Bates, sending them falling as well. There was nothing to stop them from plummeting straight to their deaths on the glacier far below!

Art Gilkey
When not climbing mountains, Gilkey was a geologist – a scientist who studies rocks.

Nothing, that is, except for Peter Schoening high above them. Schoening saw what was happening and jammed his ice pick into an opening on the rock face.

Schoening held on as hard as he could. Somehow he managed to take the strain and bring their fall to a stop, saving their lives!

But there was one tragic loss. When the team untangled the jumble of ropes and equipment and climbed upward to find Art Gilkey, he was nowhere to be seen. The impact of their fall had caused a small, localized avalanche that had swept Gilkey away.

Battered, bruised, and sad beyond words at the loss of their friend, the exhausted men slowly finished their descent.

They all knew that they were lucky to be alive after an experience that none of them would ever forget. Houston said of his team that "we entered the mountain as strangers, but left it as brothers." ❖

Memorial
A memorial cairn or stone sits at the base of K2. It commemorates the lives of Dudley Wolfe, Art Gilkey, and Sherpas who died on K2 in 1939 and 1953.

Frequent reunions
The survivors of the expedition have stayed close friends and arrange regular reunions.

This is an area of incredible natural beauty in California. It includes the famous Yosemite Valley and Falls. The Salathe Wall is part of El Capitan in the valley.

The challenge

Date: Summer, 1988
Place: The Salathe Wall, El Capitan, Yosemite Valley, California

"Are you sure this is a good idea?" asked Paul Piana, smiling.

"Too late to turn back now," answered his climbing partner, Todd Skinner. "Let's get started."

Longtime climbing friends Piana and Skinner were about to undertake their greatest challenge.

The Salathe Wall is part of El Capitan and rises 3,604 ft (1,098 m) above the valley.

They stood in front of the gray mass of granite known as El Capitan in Yosemite Valley. The tall slab of rock facing them – called the Salathe Wall – looked forbidding.

The pair were planning to climb the Salathe Wall using a technique called free-climbing. In free-climbing, ropes are only used for safety, never to pull oneself up the rock face. All the actual climbing is done using the strength of the climber's hands and feet!

No one had ever free-climbed the Salathe Wall. Would they succeed?

Piana and Skinner
Paul Piana and Todd Skinner are two of the greatest free-climbers in the world. They usually practice their climbing moves in advance. They have been the first to free-climb many dangerous mountain faces.

31

True height
The Yosemite Valley is 4,000 ft (1,212 m) above sea level and El Capitan rises another 3,604 ft (1,092 m) above the valley floor. It is the tallest monolithic rock face in the world. A monolith is a single block of stone.

Sleeping high
The men slept in portaledges – sleeping bags roped and secured to the side of the mountain. Although safe from falling in their sleep, neither man could really relax because the ground was too far away!

The first morning went well, but by the afternoon the climbing got tougher with overhanging ledges blocking their path. As twilight fell, the tired men set up camp. They were going to spend the night in sleeping bags roped to the rock face!

Piana and Skinner secured the specially designed portaledges to the rock face with reinforced straps and bolts. They then settled down for the night, hundreds of feet (meters) above ground!

The next day's climbing started early and was just as tough. As Piana and Skinner pressed on, day after day, they became more and more tired. Their hands were constantly being cut open by the rough rock face. They used their hands as anchors to help pull themselves up the rock face, so they couldn't wear protective gloves.

As they climbed higher, the rock face became a beautiful golden color and was covered by a system of cracks like a huge spider's web, but Piana didn't care what it looked like. He thrust his hand into one of the cracks to get a grip and pulled his tired body ever closer to the top.

Slippery surface
The exertion of climbing can make your hands sweat and become very slippery. A climber needs a good grip, so he coats his hands in chalk. He carries the chalk in a bag secured to his waist.

Safety lines
Climbers use incredibly strong specialist ropes. The ropes are different colors so that climbers can identify the rope they want quickly.

Piana finally felt his hand reach over the top of the rim and yanked himself up. They were safe and he was at the summit!

Piana looked around for somewhere to anchor the safety lines. He chose a huge block of heavy rock. Dozens of other climbers had used it as their safety anchor over the years.

Skinner appeared at the edge of the rim with their supply bags on another rope. He was just climbing up when there was a terrible noise behind them.

"No!" screamed Piana.

The huge rock was moving! It slid into the two friends, knocking them over the edge. Both men went spinning wildly in the air! For a long and terrible moment, Piana thought that they were both going to die.

Injuries
Their near-fatal accident left Skinner nursing an injured pelvis and having trouble breathing, and Piana hurt his left leg badly.

And down again
After they reached the top, it should have taken the pair just two hours to get down again. But because of their injuries it took them over nine hours!

But the huge block stopped moving just in time. Slowly and carefully they made their way back up to the top, knowing they were lucky to be alive. ❖

35

Roger Mear
Mear has worked as part of the British Antarctic Survey and completed many climbs in Antarctica. Today, Mear often acts as a guide for less-experienced climbers.

Sir James Clark Ross
Mount Erebus was first discovered by the explorer Sir James Clark Ross in 1841. He named the mountain after his ship, *The Erebus*.

Alone in the night

Date: June, 1985
Place: Mount Erebus, Ross Island, Antarctica

It had been dark for over a month now. Roger Mear looked out of the window of the hut. The full moon hung in the center of the sky. Its silver light shone down on the Antarctic wilderness outside.

It was time to go. Mear wanted to test himself against the desolate landscape of the South Pole. He had decided to climb Mount Erebus – an active volcano – alone.

No one had ever climbed an Antarctic mountain during the long, dark polar winter. If he survived, Roger Mear would be the first.

The first part of his journey was over the Barne Glacier – a huge expanse of solid ice. Solid, that is, except for many crevasses.

Mear strained his eyes through the moonlit gloom, looking for any signs of crevasses hidden under the snow. He was not roped to anyone, and falling down a crevasse would almost certainly mean death.

First ascent
Mount Erebus was first climbed in 1908 by an expedition led by the famous Arctic explorer Ernest Shackleton.

Mount Erebus on Ross Island is 12,448 feet high.

It took Mear seven hours of careful walking to reach the end of the glacier safely. Tired after the stressful trek, he unrolled his sleeping bag and bedded down for the night.

When Mear woke up the next morning, it was still dark. The sun would not be rising for another month! The beautiful landscape around him was strangely still and silent. Mear felt like the only man left on Earth.

Three miles later, he finally reached the base of the 12,448-ft- (3,772-m)-high Mount Erebus and began the steep climb up its slopes.

Mear knew it was important that he climb steadily and not rush. If he began to sweat, the liquid would freeze inside his clothes!

As he climbed the snow-covered side, Mear could feel himself getting colder and colder. He walked on the softer snow and avoided the hard rocks where he could to ease the ache in his legs. The climb was hard work, and Mear was soon gasping for breath.

Trouble sleeping
Mear had brought along an air mattress to sleep on. The air mattress would lift him off the ground and help to keep him warm. During the first night, he discovered a hole in the mattress and he was too cold to ever sleep well.

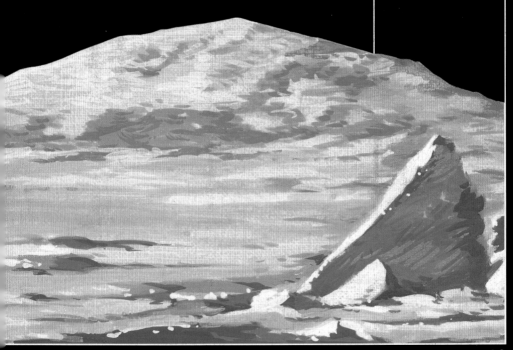

Hot and cold
The summit of Mount Erebus is continually emitting clouds of hot steam that rise from the red-hot lava pits inside the volcano's crater.

After many hours, the ground began to level out and Mear realized he was near the summit of the mountain – the volcano's crater.

At last Mear reached the edge of the crater. As he stood on the rim, he looked down 900 ft (270 m) into the inside of the volcano.

The air smelled of sulfur and clouds of steam rose from the depths. Looking through the clouds, Mear caught sight of the vast pool of red-hot lava at the volcano's base. The volcano was still active and he didn't know when it might choose to erupt.

Despite the rising steam and red hot lava inside, the volcano's walls were very thick and the outside walls were icy cold. Mear's hands were in danger of freezing, so he wasted no time in turning and heading home.

He arrived back at base, cold and tired, but he had tested himself against the harsh Antarctic winter and he had survived. ❖

Live volcano
A volcano is a crack in the Earth's surface or crust through which an incredibly hot liquid called lava can explode or erupt onto the surface.

Active volcano
When Captain Scott's expedition climbed Mount Erebus in 1912, the volcano erupted and they had to flee!

A search for heroes

Date: May, 1999
Place: Mount Everest, Himalayas,
Nepal-China border

Eric Simonson, one of the world's most experienced and respected Everest climbers, was returning to this mountain on a special mission. He was hoping to solve one of its oldest mysteries.

Andrew Irvine

George Mallory

Noel Odell

Members of the 1924 expedition photographed at base camp.

It was exactly 75 years since George Mallory and Andrew Irvine had vanished while attempting to be the first to climb Everest.

Since that fateful day in 1924, their disappearance had become a legend. Some people even thought Mallory and Irvine had made it to the summit before losing their lives on the descent.

If their bodies or camera could be found, the question might finally be answered.

Mallory's camera
Mallory was carrying a Kodak "vest pocket" camera when he disappeared. Many people wondered if it contained clues to the men's disappearance, as the extreme cold could have preserved the camera film!

Members of the 1999 expedition hoping to solve one of Everest's oldest mysteries.

Modern equipment
Specialist climbing boots and tents protect today's climbers against the cold. And improved safety features on ropes and bolts make falls less likely than in the past.

Still a killer
Even with today's technology, Everest is still a killer. In 1996, eight climbers lost their lives in one day.

Conrad Anker
Anker has climbed many of the world's most difficult mountain routes and has worked as a cameraman, making climbing films.

Simonson knew that the chances of his team finding either body in such a large and hostile area was remote. But he did have a few clues.

A 1933 expedition had found an ice axe belonging to either Mallory or Irvine. And in 1975, a Chinese climber had seen a body. When the climber touched a piece of clothing, it disintegrated in his hands, so he knew the body was very old.

Simonson's team arrived to find the weather mild and the lower mountain remarkably free of snow. This was a good omen, as earlier expeditions had met with terrible weather. Simonson's men climbed close to the height where the men were last seen.

On May 1, the team spread out and began to look for signs. About two hours into the search, Conrad Anker saw something very strange far away in the distance.

A Mallory at the summit
George Mallory may not have made it to the summit, but his grandson, George Mallory II, did in 1995.

On a snow terrace on the North Ridge, Anker spotted a tiny area of white that looked much brighter than the surrounding snow. As he approached it, he realized what he had found. With great excitement, he radioed the rest of the team to join him as fast as they could.

Three quarters of a century after Mallory had vanished, they had found his body! He had been killed during a fall from the slopes above. It was an amazing moment for all of them.

With wind blasting into their faces, the men followed the wishes of Mallory's daughter and grandsons and performed a short ceremony and then respectfully buried the body with rocks. Mallory was now at peace on his beloved mountain.

The body showed that George Mallory and Andrew Irvine had been roped together when one of them had fallen. Mallory's snow goggles were still in his pocket, suggesting the men fell in the dark. There was no trace of Irvine.

The team continued to search for the rest of the week. They found Mallory's pocket watch, but could find no trace of either Irvine's body or Mallory's camera. Perhaps there are some secrets that the mountain still wants to keep. ❖

Grave
A note about the mission of the 1999 expedition and a picture of Nepalese monks were left on Mallory's grave.

Lost camera
Most people think Mallory and Irvine never made it to the summit. Perhaps one day Mallory's camera will be found and we will find out.

Glossary

Ascent
The climb up a mountain or rock face.

Avalanche
A large mass of snow, ice, or rock that has broken loose and slides down the side of a mountain.

Blizzard
A severe snowstorm with violent winds. Blizzards often occur on the upper slopes of the world's highest mountains.

Bolt
A rod that is banged into the rock or ice on a mountain face, so a climber's safety ropes can be attached to it to prevent him from falling.

British Antarctic Survey
A scientific organization that sends people to Antarctica to study its land and animal life.

Chalk
When free-climbing, a climber needs a good grip. But sweat on a climber's hands can make them slippery. Climbers often use chalk to keep their hands dry so that they can climb better.

Crater, volcano
The mouth or open top of a volcano.

Descent
The return climb down a mountain or rock face.

Eruption, volcanic
When red-hot lava deep inside a volcano bubbles up and explodes out of the crater with force.

Frostbite
When a climber's limbs are exposed to extreme cold, his fingers can go numb, swell up, and become gray. In severe cases, the climber may lose his fingers or toes.

Glacier
A slowly moving mass of ice in a mountain valley.

Gear
Specialist climbing equipment such as bolts, chalk, and ropes.

Granite
A very hard crystalline rock found in many mountain ranges.

Lava, volcanic
Red-hot molten rock that flows from a volcano during an eruption.

Monsoon
A very strong wind. In South Asia, seasonal monsoons bring very heavy rain, which soaks everything in seconds.

Peak
The highest point or top of a mountain.

Safety anchor
Something strong and secure to which a climber attaches ropes to stop him from falling if he slips.

Safety line
Ropes used to tie climbers to each other and to safety anchors.

Snowstorm
A violent storm, usually on a mountainside, where the wind whips up large sheets of snow.

Sulfur
A pale yellow substance that burns with a blue flame and has a disagreeable smell.

Summit
The highest point or top of a mountain.

Supplies
Everything needed during an expedition, including food, clothing, climbing gear, medical supplies, and equipment to record the climb.